BACKYARD WILDLIFE

Moose

by Kristin Schuetz

ROCKFORD PUBLIC LIBRARY

BELLWETHER MEDIA • MINNEAPOLIS, MN

Note to Librarians, Teachers, and Parents:

Blastoff! Readers are carefully developed by literacy experts and combine standards-based content with developmentally appropriate text.

Level 1 provides the most support through repetition of high-frequency words, light text, predictable sentence patterns, and strong visual support.

Level 2 offers early readers a bit more challenge through varied simple sentences, increased text load, and less repetition of high-frequency words.

Level 3 advances early-fluent readers toward fluency through increased text and concept load, less reliance on visuals, longer sentences, and more literary language.

Level 4 builds reading stamina by providing more text per page, increased use of punctuation, greater variation in sentence patterns, and increasingly challenging vocabulary.

Level 5 encourages children to move from "learning to read" to "reading to learn" by providing even more text, varied writing styles, and less familiar topics.

Whichever book is right for your reader, Blastoff! Readers are the perfect books to build confidence and encourage a love of reading that will last a lifetime!

This edition first published in 2014 by Bellwether Media, Inc.

No part of this publication may be reproduced in whole or in part without written permission of the publisher. For information regarding permission, write to Bellwether Media, Inc., Attention: Permissions Department, 5357 Penn Avenue South, Minneapolis, MN 55419.

Library of Congress Cataloging-in-Publication Data

Schuetz, Kristin.
  Moose / by Kristin Schuetz.
    pages cm – (Blastoff! Readers. Backyard Wildlife)
  Summary: "Developed by literacy experts for students in kindergarten through grade three, this book introduces moose to young readers through leveled text and related photos"– Provided by publisher.
  Audience: Age 5-8.
  Audience: Grades K to 3.
  Includes bibliographical references and index.
  ISBN 978-1-60014-969-6 (hardcover : alk. paper)
  1. Moose–Juvenile literature. I. Title.
  QL737.U55S355 2014
  599.65'7–dc23
                                                                    2014001432

Printed in the United States of America, North Mankato, MN.

Contents

Moose are big **mammals**. They are the largest type of deer.

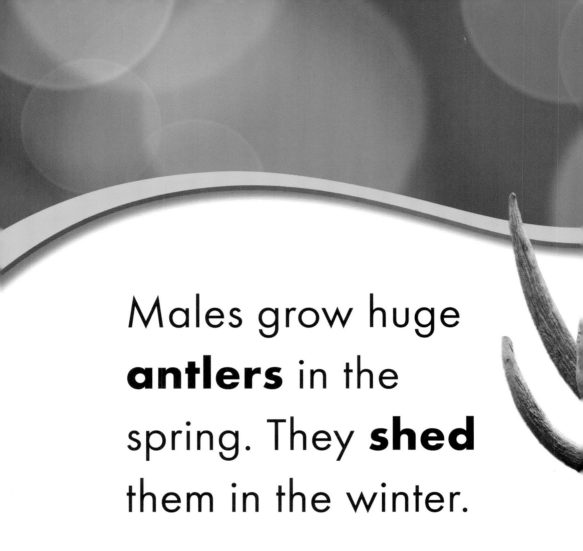

Males grow huge **antlers** in the spring. They **shed** them in the winter.

All moose have loose skin below the throat. It is called a bell.

bell

Moose walk on large **hooves**. They do not sink in mud or snow.

hoof

Moose live in forests, mountains, and **tundra**. They stay close to water.

13

Moose are great swimmers. They dip underwater to find food.

Moose eat **aquatic** plants in the summer. Winter treats are bark and twigs.

Males fight over females. They use their antlers to push one another.

Females fight **predators** to protect **calves**. A kick does the trick!

Glossary

antlers—bony, branch-like horns that grow out of a moose's head

aquatic—living in water; aquatic plants grow in water.

calves—young moose

hooves—the hard coverings that protect the feet of some animals

mammals—warm-blooded animals that have backbones and feed their young milk

predators—animals that hunt other animals for food

shed—to lose something; moose shed old antlers and grow new ones in their place.

tundra—a flat, treeless area with frozen ground

To Learn More

AT THE LIBRARY

Jeffers, Oliver. *This Moose Belongs to Me.* New York, N.Y.: Philomel Books, 2012.

Magby, Meryl. *Moose.* New York, N.Y.: PowerKids Press, 2012.

Riggs, Kate. *Moose.* Mankato, Minn.: Creative Education, 2012.

ON THE WEB

Learning more about moose is as easy as 1, 2, 3.

1. Go to www.factsurfer.com.

2. Enter "moose" into the search box.

3. Click the "Surf" button and you will see a list of related web sites.

With factsurfer.com, finding more information is just a click away.

Index

The images in this book are reproduced through the courtesy of: NHPA/ SuperStock, front cover, p. 5; Milo Burcham/ Corbis Images, p. 7; Ana Gram, p. 9; scattoselvaggio, p. 11; Tom & Pat Leeson/ Kimball Stock, p. 13 (top); Aleksey Stemmer, p. 13 (bottom left); Peter Wey, p. 13 (bottom middle); Jennifer Stone, p. 13 (bottom right); Minden Pictures/ SuperStock, pp. 15, 17 (top); Yuriy Kulik, p. 17 (bottom left); Pi-Lens, p. 17 (bottom right); Bob Gurr/ Corbis Images, p. 19; sekernas, p. 21.